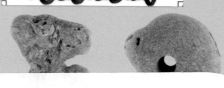

9/11

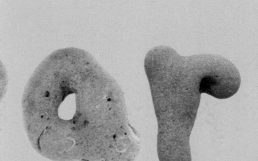

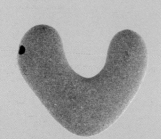

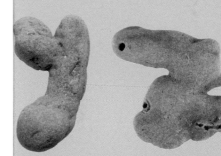

if
rocks
could
sing

if rocks

by Leslie McGuirk

COULD SING

a discovered alphabet

TRICYCLE PRESS
Berkeley

 is for **Addition**

 is for **bird**

c is for
couch potato

 is for **dog**

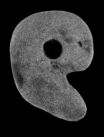 is for **elephant**

 is for **Footprint**

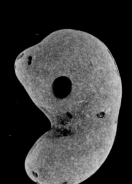 is for **ghosts**

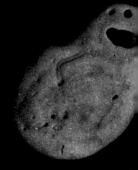

is for **holes**

 is for **igloo**

 is for **Joy**

 is for **kick**

is for **Lemon**

 is for **mitten**

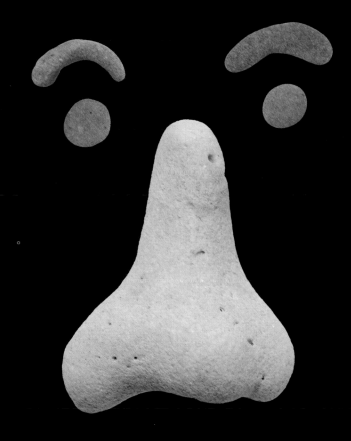

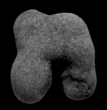 is for **nose**

 is for **Ouch**

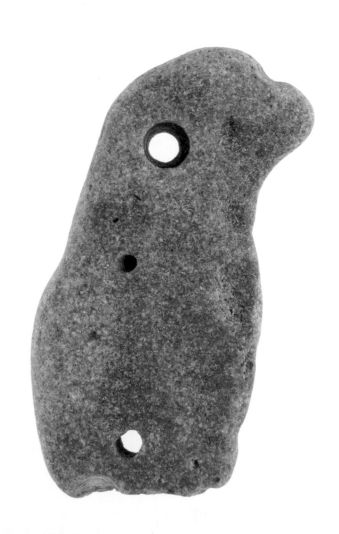

is for **Penguin**

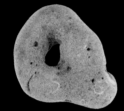

is for

Question
mark

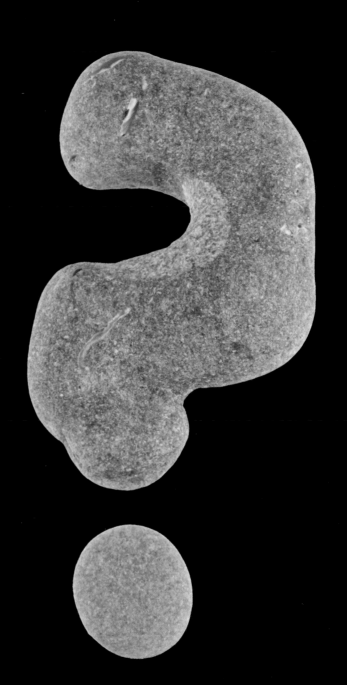

r is for **rabbit**

s is for

seahorse

 is for **Toast**

 is for **Up**

is for **Valentines**

 is for **whale**

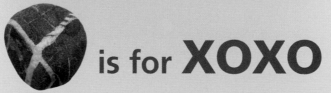

is for **XOXO**

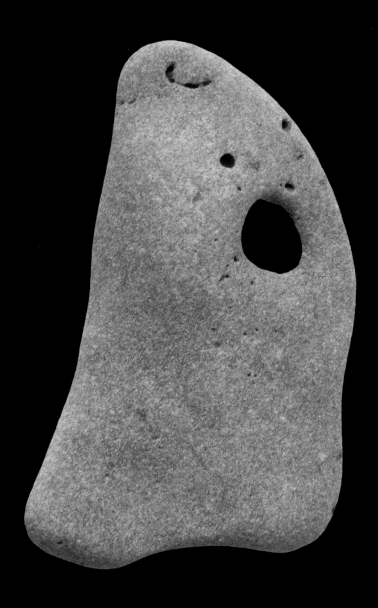

 is for **yawn**

 is for **zero**

rock talk

Vision is the art of seeing what is invisible to others.

—Jonathan Swift

This is a book born from the sea. Some people walk the beach searching for shells, all the while passing by the little rocks that make up this book.

This collection began more than ten years ago, as I discovered rocks on the Florida seashore that looked like letters. It became a real passion of mine to complete the entire alphabet. For many years, I waited for the letter K to appear. There was nothing I could do to make it show up. I understood that nature has its own timing, and my job was to be aware and expectant. The natural world is rich with inspiration. Finding these letters, and rocks that looked like objects to match them, was a process of believing that anything is possible. These are beautiful sculptures, little works of art. I feel honored to share these rocks with the world. These compositions are intended to allow these rocks to speak for themselves . . . and for us to imagine what we would hear if rocks could sing.

To my rock-solid and creatively inspired friend
Andrea Hamilton

These rocks, which are fossiliferous sandstone, contain grains of sand and fossilized shell fragments. Thousands—maybe millions—of years ago, the sand and shell fragments were deposited on the sea floor, just beyond where the waves break. Over many years, they were "glued" together by a chemical in the seawater, turning it from loose sediment into sedimentary rock. This sandstone was sculpted by being tumbled, broken, shaped, and smoothed by the waves.

The rock used for the letter X, found in Maine, was the only one not found in Florida.

Rock styling and props by Leslie McGuirk
Photographs by Denise Ritchie: www.deniseritchie.com

Library of Congress Cataloging-in-Publication Data

McGuirk, Leslie.
 If rocks could sing : a discovered alphabet / Leslie McGuirk.
 — 1st ed.
    p. cm.
 Summary: Displays photographs of rocks that resemble the letters of the alphabet and objects represented by each letter.
 [1. Rocks—Fiction. 2. Alphabet.] I. Title.
 PZ7.M4786235If 2011
 [E—dc22

                                    2010019206

ISBN 978-1-58246-370-4 (hardcover)
ISBN 978-1-58246-395-7 (Gibraltar lib. bdg.)

Printed in China

Design by Nancy Austin
The type of this book is set in Frutiger.

1 2 3 4 5 6 – 16 15 14 13 12 11

First Edition

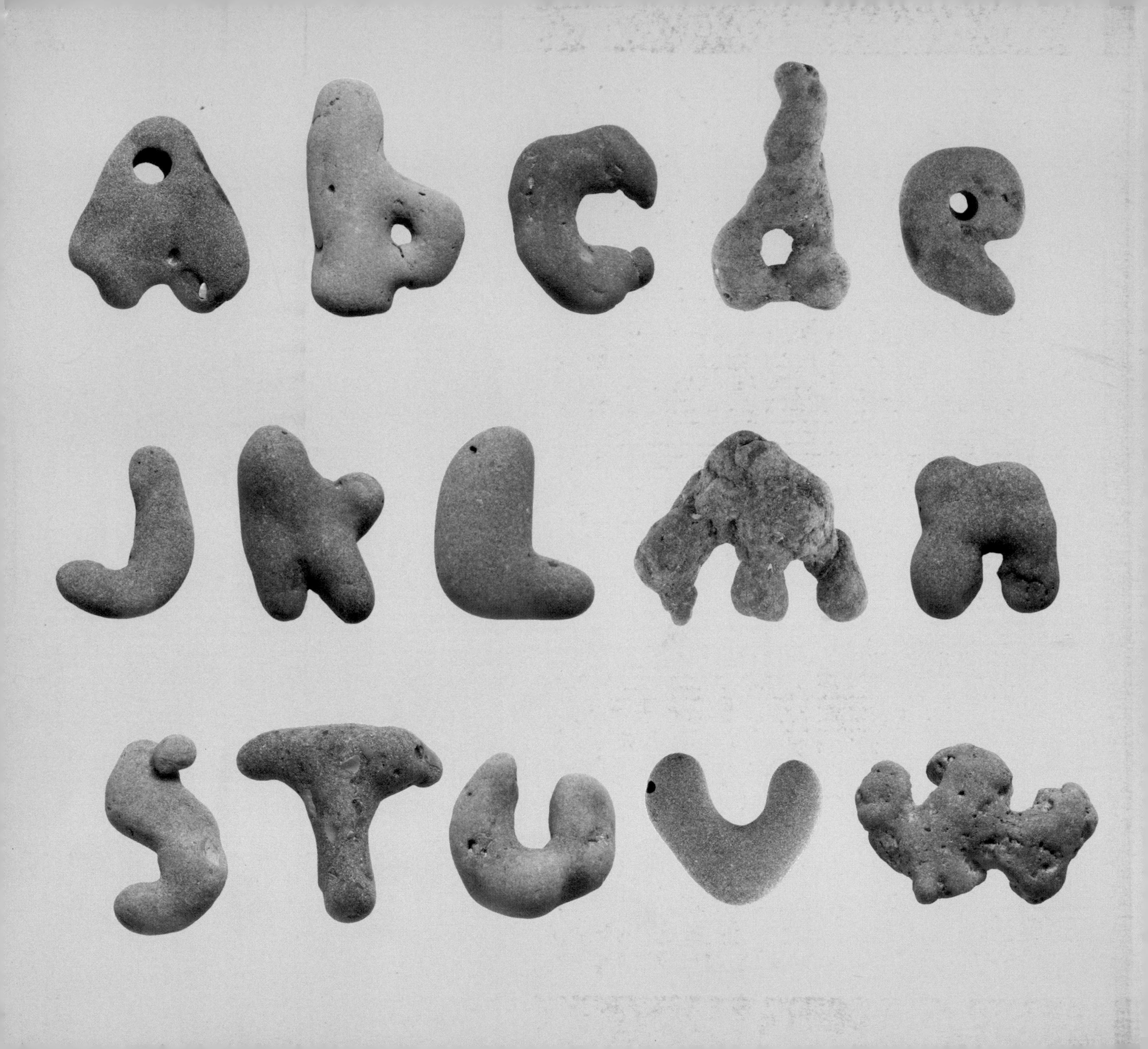